GRB

ALLEN COUNTY PUBLIC LIBRARY

FRIENDS
OF ACPL

D0699099

3 1833 04254 2990

AR Level 0.7

AR Points 0.5

Q2# 62794

Rookie reader

Soup

Written by
Cathy Goldberg Fishman

Illustrated by Ronnie Rooney

CP
Children's Press®
A Division of Scholastic Inc.
New York • Toronto • London • Auckland • Sydney
Mexico City • New Delhi • Hong Kong
Danbury, Connecticut

With love to Brittany, my inspiration
— **C.G.F.**

To my dad, who eats soup in any kind of weather
—**R.R.**

Reading Consultants

Linda Cornwell
Literacy Specialist

Katharine A. Kane
Education Consultant
(Retired, San Diego County Office of Education and San Diego State University)

Library of Congress Cataloging-in-Publication Data

Fishman, Cathy Goldberg.
  Soup/ written by Cathy Goldberg Fishman; illustrated by Ronnie Rooney.
    p. cm.—(Rookie reader)
  Summary: Each member of a family has a special job when they work together to make soup for dinner.
  ISBN 0-516-22536-7 (lib. bdg.)   0-516-26981-X (pbk.)
  [1. Soups—Fiction. 2. Family life—Fiction. 3. Stories in rhyme.] I. Rooney, Ronnie, ill. II. Title. III. Series.
PZ8.3.F63545 So 2002
[E]—dc21

                                                        2001003837

© 2002 by Children's Press®, a division of Scholastic Inc.
Illustrations © 2002 by Ronnie Rooney
All rights reserved. Published simultaneously in Canada.
Printed in the United States of America.

SCHOLASTIC and associated designs are trademarks and/or registered trademarks of Scholastic Inc. CHILDREN'S PRESS, ROOKIE READER, and A ROOKIE READER and all associated designs are trademarks and/or registered trademarks of Grolier Publishing Company, Inc.
1 2 3 4 5 6 7 8 9 10 R 11 10 09 08 07 06 05 04 03 02

When we make dinner,

3

6

Dad stirs the soup.

Watch it steam.

I put out spoons.

10

3 1833 04254 2990

Mom slices bread.

Sis puts a napkin on her head.

Dad fills four bowls.

Mom adds some cheese.

This soup is hot!

Blow gently, please.

Sis adds crackers.

25

Dad adds rice.

But when I eat soup,

I just add ice.

Word List (46 words)

a	fills	Mom	spoons
add	four	napkin	steam
adds	gently	on	stirs
blow	head	out	team
bowls	her	please	the
bread	hot	put	this
but	I	puts	watch
cheese	ice	rice	we
crackers	is	Sis	we're
Dad	it	slices	when
dinner	just	some	
eat	make	soup	

About the Author

Cathy Goldberg Fishman lives in Augusta, Georgia, with her husband, Steven, and two children, Alexander and Brittany. She grew up in Atlanta and graduated from Lesley College in Cambridge, Massachusetts. She has been a teacher, daycare director, and owner and operator of a children's bookstore. She now writes children's books. This is her first book with Children's Press.

About the Illustrator

Ronnie Rooney was born and raised in Massachusetts. She attended the University of Massachusetts in Amherst, and received her M.F.A. in illustration at Savannah College of Art and Design in Savannah, Georgia. When Ronnie isn't illustrating greeting cards or children's books, she loves to swim, run, and eat chocolate chip cookie dough. (But not all at the same time!) She lives in Plymouth, Massachusetts.